AMERICAN HEROES

GEORGE WASHINGTON

Our First President

AMERICAN HEROES

GEORGE WASHINGTON
Our First President

SNEED B. COLLARD III

mc **Marshall Cavendish**
Benchmark
New York

To Doug,
Our Founding Geezer

Marshall Cavendish Benchmark
99 White Plains Road
Tarrytown, New York 10591
www.marshallcavendish.us

Text copyright © 2010 by Sneed B. Collard III

All Internet sites were available and accurate when this book was sent to press.

Library of Congress Cataloging-in-Publication Data
Collard, Sneed B.
George Washington, our first president / by Sneed B. Collard III.
p. cm. — (American heroes)
Includes bibliographical references and index.
Summary: "A juvenile biography of the first president of the United States"—Provided by publisher.
ISBN 978-0-7614-4060-4
1. Washington, George, 1732-1799—Juvenile literature. 2. Presidents—United States—Biography—Juvenile literature. I. Title. II. Title: George Washington.
E312.66.C645 2009
973.4′1092—dc22
[B]
2008034817

Editor: Joyce Stanton
Publisher: Michelle Bisson
Art Director: Anahid Hamparian
Series Designer: Anne Scatto
Printed in Malaysia
1 3 5 6 4 2

Images provided by Debbie Needleman, Picture Researcher, Portsmouth, NH, from the following sources:
Front Cover: Private Collection/Art Resource, NY.
Back Cover: © Burstein Collection/CORBIS. *Pages i, 34:* Private Collection/Art Resource, NY; *page ii:* The Newark Museum/Art Resource, NY; *page vi:* George Washington on horseback (color litho) by American School (18th century). Private Collection/Peter Newark American Pictures/The Bridgeman Art Library; *page 1:* Signature of George Washington (ink on paper) by American School (18th century). Private Collection/Ken Welsh/The Bridgeman Art Library; *page 3:* Currier and Ives/The Bridgeman Art Library/Getty Images; *pages 5, 11, 20:* © Bettmann/CORBIS; *page 7:* George Washington in the uniform of a Colonel of the Virginia Militia during the French & Indian War (color litho) by Charles Willson Peale (1741-1827 (after). Private Collection/Peter Newark American Pictures/The Bridgeman Art Library; *page 8:* North Wind Picture Archives; *pages 12, 15, 16:* The Granger Collection, New York; *page 19:* The Philadelphia Museum of Art/Art Resource, NY; *page 23:* George Washington enters New York City 25 November 1783 (color litho) by American School (19th century). Private Collection/Peter Newark American Pictures/The Bridgeman Art Library; *page 24(top):* Library of Congress Prints and Photographs Division, Washington, D.C. (LC-USZC-4-2541); *page 24(bottom):* National Archives; *page 27:* First in War. First in Peace and First in the Hearts of his Countrymen (color litho) by American School (19th century). Collection of the New York Historical Society, USA/The Bridgeman Art Library; *page 29:* Courtesy of Mount Vernon Ladies' Association; *page 31:* Library of Congress Prints and Photographs Division, Washington, D.C. (LC-USZC4-723); *page 33:* © CORBIS

CONTENTS

George's special qualities helped make the American Revolution succeed.

G. Washington

George Washington was not the smartest man of the American Revolution. Thomas Jefferson, Benjamin Franklin, John Adams—all had better educations and, maybe, more intelligence. But George Washington had three great gifts. First, he knew how to lead. Second, he learned from his mistakes. Third, he had common sense. More than any other person, he made the American Revolution succeed.

Many stories have been told about George Washington's childhood. Almost all of these are false. The truth is that we know very little about young George. George was a private person. In later years, he rarely talked about his childhood or his parents. But we do know a few things. As a boy, George received only a few years of basic schooling. We also know that he was born in Westmoreland County, Virginia, on February 22, 1732. This was a time when Great Britain still ruled Virginia and the other twelve American colonies.

George was born in Westmoreland County, Virginia, in 1732.

As a young person, George was surrounded by rich, powerful Virginia families. George knew that he wanted this kind of life for himself. It would not be easy. When he was only eleven years old, his father died. His father left George land, but not much money. George knew he would have to work hard to succeed. When he was sixteen years old, he began work as a surveyor. For the next few years, he mapped and explored lands all over Virginia.

As a surveyor, George got the chance to explore and map lands all over Virginia.

During this time, George grew into a strong tower of a man. He stood more than six feet, two inches tall. He also learned how to live in the wilderness. In 1754, when the French tried to take over Britain's lands west of the thirteen colonies, George helped lead Virginia's troops against them. George made some poor decisions and lost a major battle. But soon, he became an expert in warfare and leading troops. In one battle, the enemy shot two horses out from under him. Bullets whistled by his head, but he continued to command his troops and keep them from being slaughtered.

As a soldier, George made many mistakes.
Unlike others, he learned from those mistakes.

George's marriage to Martha Dandridge Custis made him a wealthy man.

George quit the army in 1758. Now, he could focus on his main goal: becoming a wealthy landowner. Two things helped him out. From his older brother, he had inherited an estate called Mount Vernon. More important, he married one of Virginia's wealthiest widows. Her name was Martha Dandridge Custis. When George married Martha, he gained control of a fortune in land, money, and slaves.

Over the next sixteen years, George became one of Virginia's most important men. He and Martha spent huge amounts of money fixing up their Mount Vernon estate. George bought thousands of acres of new lands. To help him farm these lands, he also bought forty-six new slaves. When he wasn't busy with work, he hunted foxes on horseback and played cards. All in all, he was living the life of a perfect British gentleman. There was just one problem. He lived in America.

George lived the life of a British gentleman,
but trouble was brewing between America and Great Britain.

*George and many other Virginia growers were never sure
they were paid a fair price for their tobacco.*

By the mid-1700s, the relationship between Great Britain and its American colonies was growing sour. Tobacco, for instance, was one of the most important crops for Virginia farmers, but George and other large-scale growers sold their tobacco crop in Britain. George could never be sure he and other colonists were paid a fair price for what they grew.

The British also tried to make all colonists pay taxes on tea, paper goods, and other items from Britain. These taxes angered George and most other Americans. Still, George had no idea how important his role would be in the coming revolution.

In May 1775, George and other men from the thirteen colonies gathered in Philadelphia. This meeting was called the Second Continental Congress. Just a few weeks earlier, Americans had clashed with British troops in Massachusetts. The American Revolution had begun. The colonists wanted to break away from Great Britain and create their own country. To do this, they needed a real army. For those in the Continental Congress, only one person was qualified to lead that army. His name was George Washington.

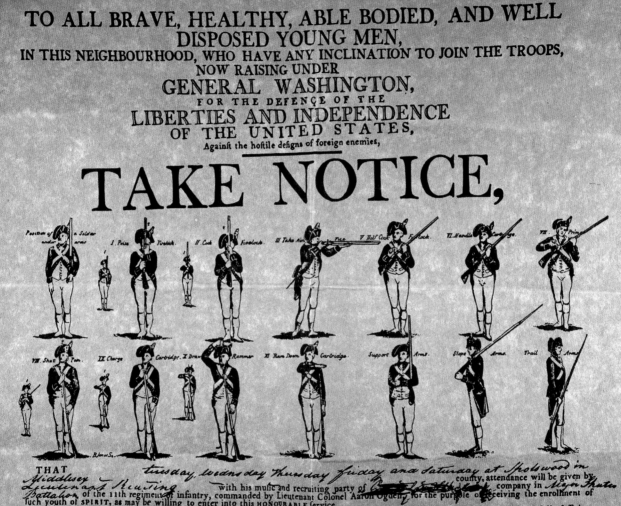

When the American Revolution began, George was chosen to lead the new army,
and advertisements were posted to recruit young men.

Thousands of British soldiers came well prepared to fight the Americans.

The war began well for the Americans. With George in charge, the army kept thousands of British troops bottled up in Boston from May 1775 until March 1776. But a few months later, the British attacked Long Island and New York City. George and his army tried to defend New York. But on the first day, the British killed 300 Americans and took more than 1,000 prisoners. That November, the British attacked Fort Washington, also in New York. This time, they captured almost 2,900 Americans and killed dozens of others.

These defeats taught George that he could not fight the British head-to-head. Instead, he had to use surprise and speed to catch them off guard. On Christmas night 1776, George led his troops across the Delaware River. At Trenton, New Jersey, the Americans surprised and defeated more than one thousand German soldiers who were being paid to fight for the British.

Sadly, the war was just beginning.

*On Christmas night 1776, George led a surprise attack on
German soldiers who were fighting for the British.*

Cold winters, a terrible diet, and disease killed more American troops than the British army did.

The fighting continued for five more hard years. Thousands of American troops died in battle. Even more died from disease. Unlike the British, the Americans were not professional soldiers. They often did not have shoes or uniforms to wear. At times, they had to eat their horses to survive. George kept the army together. He lived and fought beside his men. He scrambled to stay ahead of the British. Finally, with the help of the French navy, the Americans defeated the British at Yorktown, Virginia. The date was October 19, 1781.

The end of the war did not mean that our new nation was safe. Danger remained from both inside and outside our country. After the war, for instance, some people wanted George to use the army to take over the American government. George refused. The long war had changed him. He was no longer just looking out for his own business interests. He now firmly believed in the ideas of freedom and democracy.

The long war turned George into a true believer of democracy and freedom.

George played an important role in creating the United States Constitution.

Another danger to our new nation was a weak federal government. In every state, Americans wondered, Who was in charge of defending our country? How would the government pay its bills? Who should make new laws and deal with foreign governments? In 1787, George led a meeting called the Constitutional Convention. Here, leaders from every state decided how our government should be run, and what powers it should have. Together, they signed one of our nation's most important documents, the United States Constitution.

The Constitution states that every four years a president should be elected to lead our nation. Everyone knew who our first president should be: George Washington.

As president, George's biggest job was to forge the separate states into one *united* nation. He filled his government with the best minds in the country. He urged these men to pull our country together and solve the problems it faced. And while different people had different opinions about things, almost everyone trusted George to guide our new nation in the right direction.

As our first president, George worked to pull the separate states into one strong nation.

One of the most important decisions George made was to serve only two terms as president. Kings and dictators ruled their countries for as long as they lived. George believed that in a free nation, leaders should not serve too long. So, after eight years as president, he retired from government and returned to Mount Vernon. He looked forward to a peaceful life as a private citizen and farmer. The new nation, though, would not leave him alone.

After eight years as president, George looked forward to
a peaceful life at Mount Vernon.

After he left the government, George still got tangled up in politics. Americans disagreed, just as we do today, on many issues. Each group wanted George on its side. There was one issue, though, that loomed over all the others: the question of slavery.

Like many famous Americans at that time, George owned other human beings as slaves. During his life, he came to believe that this was wrong. As president, he did not think he could convince the nation to end slavery. But he did come up with a plan to free his own slaves.

George was torn by the issue of slavery
but did not think the nation was ready to make slavery illegal.

Unfortunately, George died before he could carry out his plan. One day, he became ill after riding his horse in a winter storm. The illness took his life on December 14, 1799. He left a will, however, in which he said that after his death his slaves would be free. It was not a perfect solution, but for a few slaves at least, it was a beginning.

The same could be said about the United States. It wasn't a perfect nation, but it had begun. And for that, we thank the leadership and common sense of our first president—George Washington.

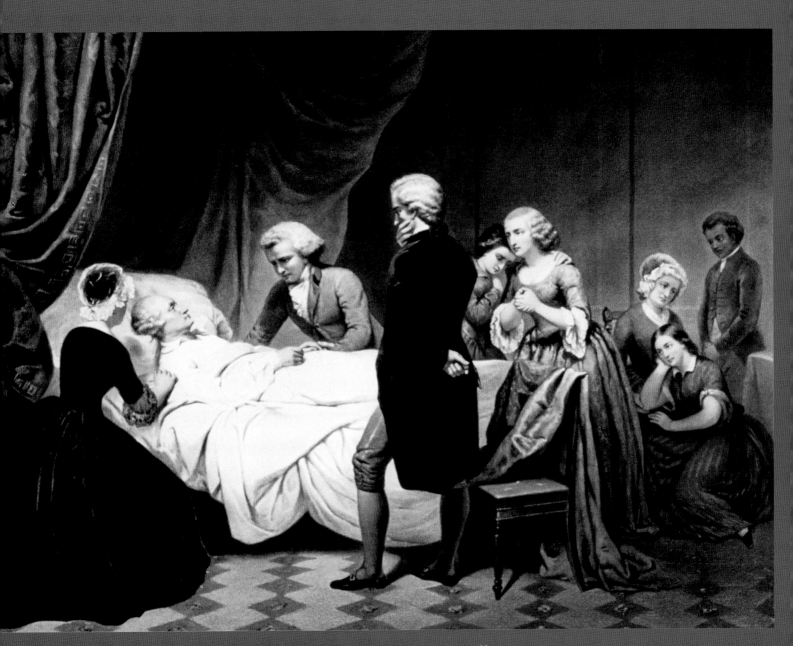

George died quickly and unexpectedly.
By his wishes, his slaves were freed after his death.

IMPORTANT DATES

1732 Born February 22 in Westmoreland County, Virginia.

1743 Father, Augustine Washington, dies.

1752 Inherits Mount Vernon from Lawrence Washington, his brother.

1754 Leads Virginia troops into battle against the French.

1759 Marries Martha Dandridge Custis.

1775 First shots of the American Revolution fired at Lexington and Concord in Massachusetts.

1775 Travels to Second Continental Congress in Philadelphia; chosen to lead the Continental Army.

1781 With the help of France, defeats British in the Battle of Yorktown.

1789 Elected first president of the United States.

1797 Steps down as president after two four-year terms.

1799 Dies at Mount Vernon on December 14 of a throat infection.

WORDS TO KNOW

American Revolution (also called the Revolutionary War or the War for Independence) The war the American colonies fought to win freedom from Great Britain. The war was fought from 1775 to 1781. A peace treaty was officially signed in 1783.

colonist A person who lives in a colony.

colony A territory that is ruled by another country. A colony is often far away from the country that governs it.

Continental Congress An early governing body set up by the thirteen colonies before they won independence from Great Britain; also the name of the meetings the colonial leaders held.

democracy A government that is run by the people. The people may elect representatives who govern for them. Or they may run the government directly by having meetings that everyone may attend.

estate A large property, usually consisting of a big house and acres of land.

independence Freedom from the control of others.

inherit To receive something from someone who has died.

politics The different ideas and opinions of how a government should be run.

slave A person who is owned by another person.

surveyor Someone who explores and maps lands, and fixes borders and property lines.

taxes Money that people must pay the government. Governments often charge people taxes on goods they buy, money they earn, or property they own.

To Learn More about George Washington

WEB SITES

George Washington
http://www.enchantedlearning.com/history/us/pres/washington/

Mount Vernon
http://www.mountvernon.org/

Rediscovering George Washington
http://www.pbs.org/georgewashington/

The White House
http://www.whitehouse.gov/history/presidents/gw1.html

BOOKS

George Washington by Cheryl Harness. National Geographic Society, 2006.

George Washington: Soldier, Hero, President by Justine Korman. DK Publishing, 2001.

George Washington, Spymaster: How the Americans Outspied the British and Won the Revolutionary War by Thomas B. Allen. National Geographic Society, 2004. (This is a longer book, but well worth the effort!)

George Washington's Teeth by Deborah Chandra and Madeleine Comora. Farrar, Straus and Giroux, 2003.

PLACES TO VISIT

George Washington Birthplace National Monument
1732 Popes Creek Road
Washington's Birthplace, VA 22443
PHONE: (804) 224-1732 WEB SITE: **http://www.nps.gov/gewa/**

Historic Mount Vernon
3200 Mount Vernon Memorial Highway
Mount Vernon, VA 22121
PHONE: (703) 780-2000
WEB SITE: **http://www.mount vernon.org/index.cfm**

Valley Forge National Park
1400 North Outer Line Drive
King of Prussia, PA 19406
PHONE: (610) 783-1077 WEB SITE: **http://www.nps.gov/vafo/**

Washington Monument National Memorial
National Mall
Washington, DC
PHONE: (202) 426-6841 WEB SITE: **http://www.nps.gov/wamo/**

INDEX

Page numbers for illustrations are in boldface.

About the Author

SNEED B. COLLARD III is the author of more than fifty award-winning books for young people, including *Science Warriors*; *Wings*; *Pocket Babies*; and the four-book SCIENCE ADVENTURES series for Marshall Cavendish Benchmark. In addition to his writing, Sneed is a popular speaker and presents widely to students, teachers, and the general public. In 2006, he was selected as the Washington Post–Children's Book Guild Nonfiction Award winner for his achievements in children's writing. He is also the author of several novels for young adults, including *Dog Sense*, *Flash Point*, and *Double Eagle*. To learn more about Sneed, you can visit his Web site at www.sneedbcollardiii.com.